D1258759

Nuclear Meltdowns

PETER BENOIT

Children's Press®
An Imprint of Scholastic Inc.
New York   Toronto   London   Auckland   Sydney
Mexico City   New Delhi   Hong Kong
Danbury, Connecticut

Content Consultant
Richard S. Fiske, PhD
Geologist Emeritus
Smithsonian Institution
Washington, DC

Library of Congress Cataloging-in-Publication Data

Benoit, Peter, 1955–
  Nuclear meltdowns/Peter Benoit.
    p. cm.—(A true book)
  Includes bibliographical references and index.
    ISBN-13: 978-0-531-25422-6 (lib. bdg.)   ISBN-13: 978-0-531-26627-4 (pbk.)
    ISBN-10: 0-531-25422-4 (lib. bdg.)   ISBN-10: 0-531-26627-3 (pbk.)
    1. Nuclear power plants—Accidents—Juvenile literature. 2. Nuclear energy—Safety measures—
  Juvenile literature. I. Title. II. Series.
  TK9152.B4265 2012
  363.17'99—dc22   2011007142

All rights reserved. Published in 2012 by Children's Press, an imprint of Scholastic Inc.
Printed in China 62
SCHOLASTIC, CHILDREN'S PRESS, A TRUE BOOK, and associated logos are trademarks and/or registered trademarks of Scholastic Inc.
8 9 10 R 21 20 19 18 17

Scholastic Inc., 557 Broadway, New York, NY 10012.

Find the Truth!

Everything you are about to read is true *except* for one of the sentences on this page.

Which one is **TRUE**?

T or F Tens of thousands of people fled after the Chernobyl meltdown.

T or F The United States does not use nuclear power anymore.

Find the answers in this book.

Contents

THE **BIG** TRUTH!

Japan's Nuclear Crisis

5 Nuclear Future?

Uranium glass is also known as vaseline glass.

Burning fossil fuels, such as the coal used in this power plant, releases harmful gases into the air.

Fossil fuels supply about 90 percent of the world's electricity.

CHAPTER 1

Taming the Atom

Our lives would be very different without electricity. But generating power can come with challenges. Most electricity is generated by burning **fossil fuels** such as coal, petroleum, and natural gas. These fuels give off the gases carbon dioxide, sulfur dioxide, and nitrogen oxide. The latter two combine with water vapor to create acid rain. This is a type of pollution that kills fish and adds acid to soil. Acid rain can even erode concrete! Carbon dioxide may contribute to climate change by trapping heat from the sun near Earth's surface.

Nuclear energy is an alternative source of electricity. Nuclear power plants create electricity without adding large amounts of harmful gases to the atmosphere. But these power plants have two drawbacks. One, they are expensive to build. And two, when they generate electricity, they create **radioactive** materials. These materials create **radiation**. A certain level of radiation surrounds us in the natural world and is harmless. But high levels of radiation, if released into the air, damage the health of living creatures. This damage can last for decades.

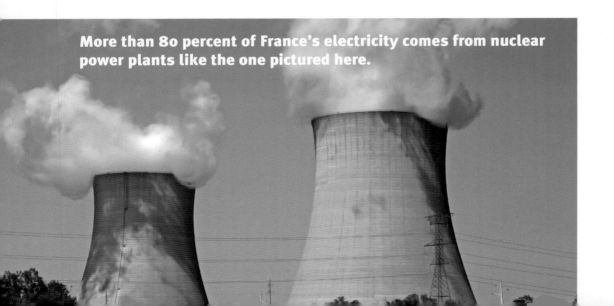

More than 80 percent of France's electricity comes from nuclear power plants like the one pictured here.

Enrico Fermi won the Nobel Prize in Physics in 1938.

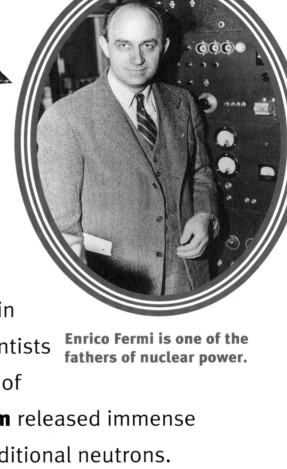

Enrico Fermi is one of the fathers of nuclear power.

Inventing Nuclear Power

Italian scientist Enrico Fermi discovered that **neutrons** could split certain kinds of atoms. Other scientists found that splitting atoms of an **element** called **uranium** released immense amounts of energy and additional neutrons. Under certain circumstances, scientists thought, the energy could be controlled in a specially constructed **reactor**. On December 2, 1942, a team led by Fermi created a successful reactor at the University of Chicago.

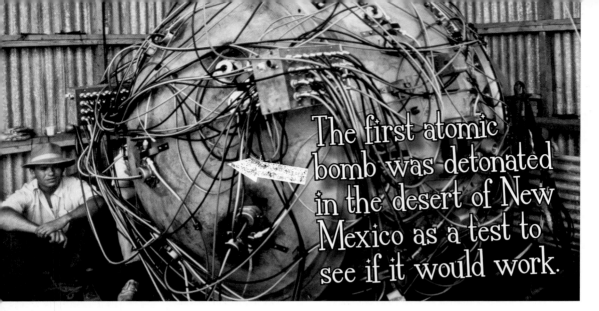

The first atomic bomb was detonated in the desert of New Mexico as a test to see if it would work.

The world's first atomic bomb was detonated on July 16, 1945.

Early work on splitting atoms, or **fission**, focused on building weapons such as the atomic bombs used in World War II. After the war, the U.S. government created the Atomic Energy Commission. It explored using nuclear technology in peaceful ways. In 1951, scientists first generated electricity with nuclear fission in Idaho. Throughout the 1950s, the government increasingly gave private companies the once-secret nuclear technology to produce electricity.

How a Reactor Works

The core of a reactor is made up of thousands of thin metal fuel rods. These rods contain uranium. Inside a reactor, neutrons break apart the **nuclei**, or centers, of the uranium atoms. The pieces of the nuclei are known as fission products. The fission products collide with other nuclei. That produces heat. The fission process repeats countless times. Technicians can control how fast fission takes place by inserting additional metal rods, called control rods, into the core.

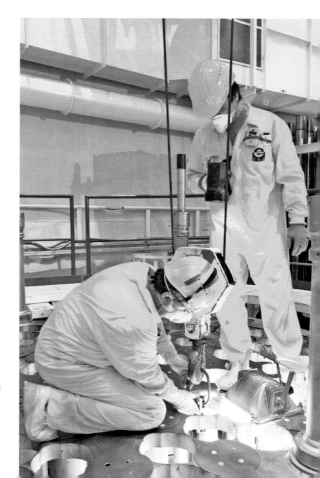

Nuclear technicians wear protective gear while they are working.

Technicians further control fission by controlling the temperature of water that moves through the reactor core. The water slows down neutrons, and slower neutrons are more effective at fission. Water also cools the core. Pumps, meanwhile, send the water through two sets of pipes. The primary loop of pipe heats the water in another, secondary loop. This produces steam that then turns a machine called a turbine. As the turbine spins, it creates energy that another machine, the generator, changes into electricity.

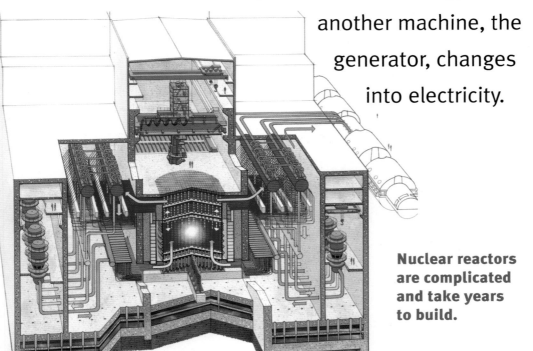

Nuclear reactors are complicated and take years to build.

California's San Onofre Nuclear Generating Station can power 1.5 million homes.

Containment buildings are some of the strongest structures on Earth.

The Containment Building

A container called a reactor vessel surrounds the core. Several feet of steel or steel-reinforced concrete—called the containment building—surround the vessel, the primary loop, and other machinery. The containment building protects the core of the reactor where dangerous overheating could take place. Laws state that it must be strong enough to withstand disasters of all kinds, such as hurricanes or tornadoes. If the core becomes too hot, the containment building is designed to help confine the dangers of overheating to a small area.

The meltdown at Chernobyl caused severe damage to the power plant.

Meltdown

A **meltdown** occurs if the fuel in the reactor core gets so hot that it begins to melt. The core can overheat when there's not enough water to cool the reactor. The coolant might stop moving around the core fast enough to carry away the heat. The water in the core may boil. It might also leak. When any of these things happen, a dangerous steam bubble may form around the fuel and prevent the core from cooling properly.

The Chernobyl nuclear power station in Ukraine had four reactors.

Nuclear plants have safety systems to prevent meltdowns. A reactor automatically shuts down whenever a water leak develops or water temperature gets too high.

The Kashiwazaki-Kariwa power plant in Tokyo is the largest nuclear plant in the world.

In 2007, Japan's Kashiwazaki-Kariwa power plant was shut down temporarily after its safety systems failed during an earthquake.

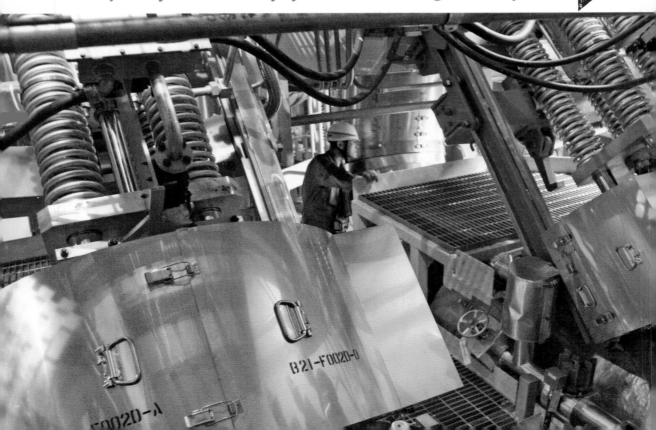

Technicians carefully monitor all the reactor's systems.

This prompts emergency cooling systems to activate and automatically cool the core. Even when an emergency shutdown occurs, workers at the plant may still have to hurry to cool the reactor. A complete core meltdown is considered the worst nuclear plant disaster. A melted core could burn its way through the containment building's floor. If it did, dangerous radioactive material might be released into the soil and water.

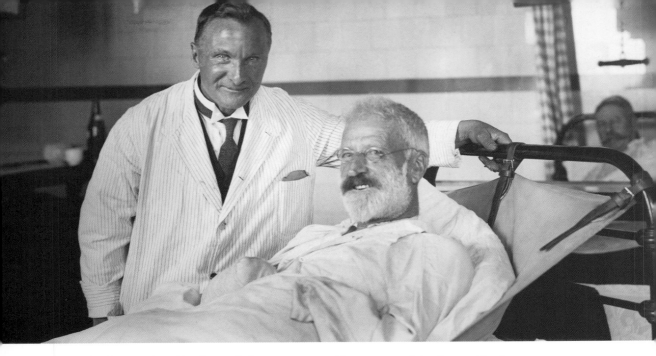

Victims of radiation sickness sometimes need to have their limbs amputated.

Radiation Sickness

Radiation in small doses has no health effects. We get small doses when we get an X-ray, for instance. But radiation in very high doses causes very serious illness or death. Symptoms include severe headaches, vomiting, and internal bleeding. A victim's hair falls out, and the skin develops blisters and sores. Death often follows.

A lower dose of radiation produces milder symptoms and allows for a better chance of survival. But even then, exposure can have long-lasting effects. Radiation increases the likelihood of tumors and certain kinds of cancer. Worse, the effects may not show up for 30 years or more. How radiation affects a person depends on the kind of radiation, the dose, and how it gets into the body.

Some Russian clinics specialize in treating radiation sickness.

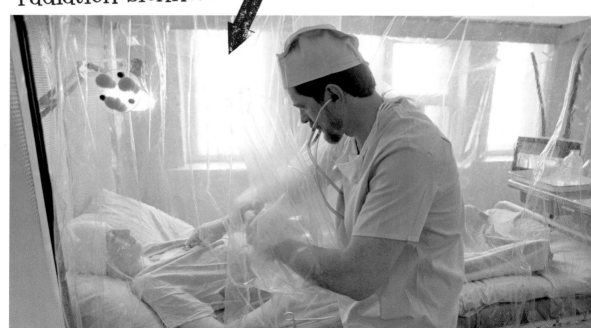

USS *Enterprise* was the first aircraft carrier to be powered by a nuclear reactor.

Nuclear Becomes Popular

Despite the risks, in the 1970s nuclear plants played an increasing role in meeting U.S. energy needs. Why? For one thing, the technology seemed safe. Nuclear reactors even powered ships. Because the reactors were located right on the ships, there was no need to stop at a port to fill up with oil or coal. This meant an aircraft carrier such as the USS *Enterprise* could remain at sea for months. By 1979, 72 reactors provided 12 percent of U.S. commercial (nongovernment) electricity. But the same year, an accident in Pennsylvania shocked the public and raised fears about nuclear safety.

Uranium

Uranium is a radioactive metal. It is also unusually heavy. A piece of uranium the size of a 1-gallon (3.8 liter) container weighs more than 150 pounds (68 kilograms). In the Middle Ages, craftspeople in what today is the Czech Republic used it to color glass yellow or certain shades of green. The discovery of radioactivity in 1896 eventually led to the research of scientists such as Enrico Fermi. Their work led to uranium becoming a source of today's nuclear fuel.

The accident at Three Mile Island changed the way people thought about nuclear power in the United States.

PENNSYLVANIA

Lake Erie

NY

MA

CT

NJ

Three Mile Island ☢

OH

MD

DE

Washington, D.C.

ATLANTIC OCEAN

WV

VA

NC

0   50 MI

Three Mile Island

The most severe nuclear accident in U.S. history took place at the Three Mile Island (TMI) nuclear plant near Harrisburg, Pennsylvania, on March 28, 1979. At around 4 a.m., the secondary loop water pumps in Unit 2 suddenly stopped working. Systems detected the problem and automatically shut down the reactor. But water pressure kept rising in the primary system of pipes. Automated systems opened a valve and relieved the pressure.

After TMI's accident, 7 similar power plants were shut down for safety inspections.

Heat at the Core

The valve was supposed to close after the pressure eased. It did not. The operator's instruments also failed to tell him it was still open. Coolant rushed out of the open valve in the primary loop. The core, deprived of coolant, began to get hotter. Emergency core-cooling pumps had come on. But, unaware of the open valve and the leaking coolant, technicians shut down the pumps so that the primary loop wouldn't overfill. The mistake allowed temperatures in the core to rise above the danger level.

After the accident, federal officials toured the plant to inspect its safety equipment.

Control panels were supposed to give Three Mile Island's technicians the information they needed to prevent a meltdown.

About half of the core melted during the accident at Three Mile Island.

Alarms sounded. Warning lights flashed. The technicians had no idea that a loss-of-coolant meltdown was in progress. Temperatures of 5,000 degrees Fahrenheit (2,760 degrees Celsius) broke the metal tubes holding the nuclear fuel. Half the uranium fuel in the core melted in a short period of time. Small amounts of radioactive gas escaped into the atmosphere.

People in the area of Three Mile Island were evacuated to shelters.

General Emergency

At 6:56 a.m., a plant official announced a general emergency. This is a warning that radiation could threaten the surrounding community. The government learned of the problem at 8:00 a.m. Inspectors immediately rushed to the scene. At 11 a.m., all but essential staff evacuated Three Mile Island. About the same time, helicopters hired by the government and TMI's owners began testing the air for radioactivity.

Sixteen hours after the accident, TMI operators discovered the coolant problem. Pumping water through the primary loop soon dropped the reactor's temperature. But by then, the core had mostly melted. Still, the emergency seemed over. Then, on March 30, a bubble of hydrogen appeared in the reactor vessel that held the core. Officials worried that if the flammable gas exploded, the core might be blown through the containment building floor and dump radioactive waste into the ground.

After the meltdown, scientists continually monitored radiation levels in the surrounding area.

About two million people were in the area of Three Mile Island when the meltdown occurred.

Public Reaction

The public began to hear news accounts of the accident and panicked. On March 30, area schools closed, government officials told people to stay inside, and farmers brought their animals indoors for protection. Pennsylvania governor

Governor Thornburgh had been in office for 68 days when the Three Mile Island meltdown occurred.

Dick Thornburgh asked pregnant women and preschool children within 5 miles (8 kilometers) of TMI to evacuate. More than 140,000 people decided to leave. Later investigations showed that too little radiation had escaped to cause health problems, though not everyone believed the test results.

It took 14 years to clean up Three Mile Island.

Many people rallied for Three Mile Island to be shut down permanently.

Technicians solved the hydrogen problem. The emergency was over, but the accident damaged the public's view of nuclear power. They no longer felt safe living near nuclear plants. People also believed that the $975 million required to clean up TMI was a high price to pay.

Many Chernobyl cleanup workers later died from radiation exposure.

The Soviet government hired workers to clean up after the Chernobyl disaster.

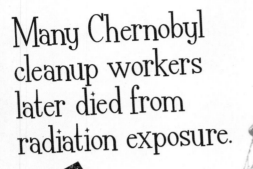

CHAPTER 4

Disaster at Chernobyl

Three Mile Island was a scare, but nobody was hurt. What happened at Chernobyl was the real thing. On April 26, 1986, workers at the Chernobyl Nuclear Power Plant near Pripyat, Ukraine, were testing the site's Number Four reactor. A sudden power surge caused by design problems exposed hot fuel to the coolant. The resulting steam explosion caused the reactor vessel to break. Unlike reactors in the Western world, these Russian reactors weren't inside a containment building.

A series of steam explosions followed, flinging radioactive fuel and pieces of the core into the atmosphere. Smoke from the resulting fires then carried a **fallout** cloud over Pripyat.

Firefighters tried to keep the flames from reaching the nearby Number Three reactor. On the afternoon of April 27, authorities ordered Pripyat residents to leave. The evacuees were told they could return in three days. Tens of thousands of other people in nearby areas had to move as well.

Timeline of Nuclear Power History

1942
The first successful nuclear reactor is built.

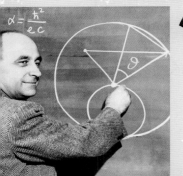

1951
An Idaho reactor generates electricity.

1955
The USS *Nautilus* becomes the world's first nuclear-powered submarine.

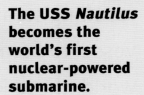

Inside Chernobyl

As the reactor fuel and other material melted, it started to burn through the building's concrete floor. A tunnel and two floors containing pools of water for coolant were below the reactor. Once the superheated fuel struck the water, it caused a steam explosion. This added more harmful radioactive material to the air. Three firefighters dove into the water and successfully opened valves to drain the water. They all later developed radiation sickness.

1986
The Chernobyl reactor melts down.

1979
The Three Mile Island accident occurs.

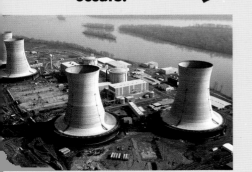

2011
Japanese nuclear reactors are damaged by earthquake and tsunami.

Some scientists feared that radioactivity from Chernobyl would spread as far as England.

Scientists used special filters to measure radioactivity in the air.

The Secret Gets Out

Chernobyl released far more radiation than Three Mile Island did. The day of the accident, fallout set off alarms at a Swedish nuclear plant 700 miles (1,127 km) away. Eventually, the radioactive cloud reached countries from Turkey to Ireland. The Soviet Union had covered up the accident when it happened. But on April 29, the government admitted an accident had taken place. European governments feared that milk and certain crops had been poisoned by the radioactive material. They put restrictions on eating those foods.

Uncertain Numbers

Between 30 and 50 rescue workers and Chernobyl technicians were killed responding to the emergency or by radiation sickness in the weeks that followed. Since then, no one knows how many people have died of radiation-related cancer or other diseases. A United Nations study put the number of deaths at 56 and predicted that 4,000 would eventually die as a result of the disaster.

People leaving the Soviet Union were checked for radiation.

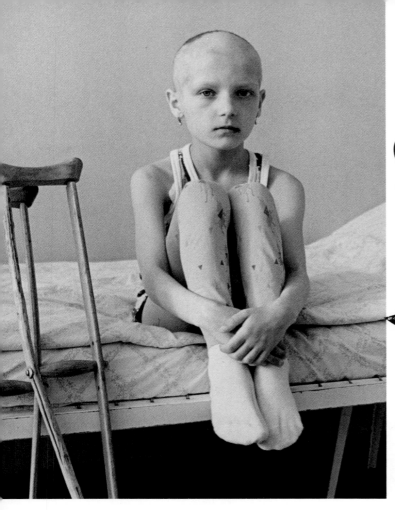

Chernobyl released more radiation into the air than an atomic bomb does.

People who were near Chernobyl during the meltdown suffered severe burns.

Ongoing Health Problems

Opinions are divided on the problems caused by the fallout. Studies have suggested high rates of thyroid cancer and other problems have occurred among those people exposed. Other studies disagree.

Inside the Disaster Zone

Despite a governmental ban, several hundred people have returned to live in the area around the plant. A few hundred evacuees, many of them older people, returned to their villages. Others, some of them homeless, have made homes in deserted and crumbling buildings. Radiation levels have fallen enough so that tourists can visit Pripyat and the nearby Red Forest. In late 2010, the Ukraine government announced that the Chernobyl power plant would open for tours.

THE BIG TRUTH!

Japan's Nuclear Crisis

On March 11, 2011, a massive earthquake occurred just off the coast of Japan. The earthquake caused waves over 65 feet (20 meters) tall to travel miles inland. The waves destroyed entire towns. They also created problems at several nuclear power plants. Workers at these plants braved high radiation levels to help prevent meltdowns from occurring. It will be years before scientists fully understand the events at these plants and their long-term effects.

Earthquake's epicenter

Sea of Japan (East Sea)

Sendai

Tokyo

JAPAN

Fukushima Daiichi

PACIFIC OCEAN

JAPAN   U.S.

PACIFIC OCEAN

0   50 MI

Fukushima I

Radiation levels around the Fukushima I plant soared after its cooling system stopped working. Three of its six reactors experienced problems. By late April, everyone living within 31 miles (50 km) of the plant was evacuated.

Fukushima II

Cooling problems also affected the Fukushima II plant. The problem was corrected fairly soon after the earthquake. The plant's systems cooled down all four reactors in just over three weeks.

Rokkasho

Rokkasho Reprocessing Plant extracts reusable material from used nuclear fuel. This means a large amount of used nuclear fuel is stored there. People feared that this fuel could catch fire if the plant's cooling system stopped working.

Nuclear waste is placed in special containers and stored in specially designed buildings.

SWB0203
TP-192

USA DOT 7A TYPE A
RADIOACTIVE MATERIAL
MFG. PETERSEN INC.
1527 NORTH 2000 WEST
OGDEN, UTAH 84404
PO 00038880

USA DOT 7A TYPE A
RADIOACTIVE MATERIAL
MFG. PETERSEN INC.
1527 NORTH 2000 WEST
OGDEN, UTAH 84404
PO 00038880

CHAPTER 5

Nuclear Future?

Today, 104 nuclear plants supply electricity to the United States. The oldest ones have been in operation since before 1979. No new sites have opened since Three Mile Island. Fear of meltdowns is not the only concern. A reactor's used-up fuel rods remain radioactive for thousands of years. Storing the used-up rods is a problem because no one wants nuclear waste near their homes. Many plants store waste on their sites because there is nowhere else to put it.

← About 2,535 tons of nuclear waste are created each year.

Worries about climate change related to fossil fuels have brought back interest in nuclear power. People may soon face a choice about whether to continue using fossil fuels as our main power source. Nuclear power could once again become a popular option. ★

More and more people are becoming concerned about the gases released into the air by burning fossil fuels.

True Statistics

Number of U.S. reactors using water as a coolant: 104

Temperature in the core at Three Mile Island: 5,000°F (2,760°C)

Number of people who evacuated TMI area: More than 140,000

Cost of cleaning up TMI Unit 2: $975 million

Time it took Soviet government to release news of Chernobyl: 3 days

Death toll at Chernobyl, according to United Nations: 56

Official population of Pripyat, Ukraine, in 2011: 0

Percentage of U.S. power supplied by nuclear plants in 2011: 19.6 percent

Number of nuclear plants worldwide in 2011: 441

Did you find the truth?

(T) Tens of thousands of people fled after the Chernobyl meltdown.

(F) The United States does not use nuclear power anymore.

Resources

Books

Adams, Troon H. *Nuclear Energy: Power From the Atom*. New York: Crabtree, 2010.

Bankston, John. *Enrico Fermi and the Nuclear Reactor*. Hockessin, DE: Mitchell Lane, 2003.

Cole, Michael D. *Three Mile Island: Nuclear Disaster*. Berkeley Heights, NJ: Enslow, 2002.

Feigenbaum, Aaron. *Emergency at Three Mile Island*. New York: Bearport, 2007.

Hantula, Richard. *Nuclear Power*. New York: Chelsea Clubhouse, 2010.

Lassieur, Allison. *Marie Curie: A Scientific Pioneer*. New York: Franklin Watts, 2003.

Levete, Sarah. *Nuclear Power*. New York: Franklin Watts, 2007.

Morris, Neil. *Nuclear Power*. New York: Franklin Watts, 2009.

Parker, Vic. *Chernobyl 1986*. Chicago: Heinemann-Raintree, 2006.

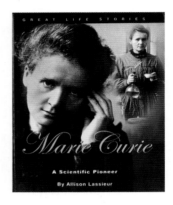

Organizations and Web Sites

American Experience: Meltdown at Three Mile Island

www.pbs.org/wgbh/amex/three/filmmore/index.html

Read interviews with experts and eyewitnesses talking about the events at Three Mile Island.

Smithsonian National Museum of American History— Three Mile Island: The Inside Story

http://americanhistory.si.edu/tmi

Study the emergency at Three Mile Island with articles, maps, illustrations, and other resources.

Places to Visit

Chernobyl Power Plant Tour

SoloEast Travel
#10 Proreznaya St.
Office #105
Kiev, Ukraine
380 44 406-3500
www.tourkiev.com/chernobyltour
See history up close with a tour of the Chernobyl region that includes the power plant, Pripyat, and the famous Red Forest.

Los Alamos Historical Museum

1050 Bathtub Row
Los Alamos, NM 87544
(505) 662-4493
www.losalamoshistory.org/Museum.htm
Walk through the once secret city of Los Alamos, home to the scientific project that advanced nuclear research and created the atomic bomb.

Important Words

element (EL-uh-muhnt)—a substance that cannot be divided up into simpler substances

fallout (FAWL-out)—radioactive particles that fall from the atmosphere

fission (FISH-uhn)—the splitting of an atom

fossil fuels (FOSS-uhl FYOO-uhl)—fuels that are naturally formed below Earth's surface

meltdown (MELT-doun)—the accidental melting of a nuclear reactor core

neutrons (NOO-trahnz)—one of the extremely small parts that form the nucleus of an atom

nuclear energy (NOO-klee-ur EN-ur-jee)—energy released from the nucleus of an atom

nuclei (NOO-klee-eye)—plural of nucleus, the center of an atom

radiation (ray-dee-AY-shuhn)—atomic particles that are sent out from a radioactive substance

radioactive (ray-dee-oh-AK-tiv)—containing particles released by nuclear energy

reactor (ree-AK-tur)—a device in which nuclear energy is produced by splitting atoms under controlled conditions

uranium (yur-AY-nee-uhm)—a radioactive element that serves as fuel in nuclear power plants

Index

Page numbers in **bold** indicate illustrations

About the Author

Peter Benoit is educated as a mathematician but has many other interests. He has taught and tutored high school and college students for many years, mostly in math and science. He also runs summer workshops for writers and students of literature. Mr. Benoit has also written more than 2,000 poems. His life has been one committed to learning. He lives in Greenwich, New York.